WORKBOOK PRESS LLC
187 E Warm Springs Rd,
Suite B285, Las Vegas, NV 89119, USA

Website: https://workbookpress.com/
Hotline: 1-888-818-4856
Email: admin@workbookpress.com

Ordering Information:
Quantity sales. Special discounts are available on quantity purchases by corporations, associations, and others.
For details, contact the publisher at the address above.

ISBN-13:   978-1-956876-38-3 (Paperback Version)
                      978-1-956876-39-0 (Digital Version)

REV. DATE: 17/11/2021

"Whoever lives in love lives in God, and God in them."

On a beautiful spring morning, nestled near a meadow creek, a little goose named Odette hatched from her egg. She has four other siblings that hatched before her. One by one, they come out from their eggs happily chirping away.. and the mother goose was so excited until all their feathers dried up.

Momma Goose was dismayed because Little Odette is different in color. Odette was black! Her other chicks are cute little yellow gooselings, but Odette was not. Momma Goose's friends laughed at her and said that Odette is an odd little one. They talked behind her back and was worried that Odette might bring bad luck to the flock!

omma Goose was ashamed and scared so she took Odette to the chicken coup and left her there to a hen's care. Mother Hen took Odette without hesitation! She said, she will take good care of Odette and raise her like her own. Momma Goose thanked Mother Hen and then left.

Mother Hen is not like any other hen. She is brave and kind and is always busy taking care of all the eggs and chicks in her coup. She even takes care of other stray animals, specially the young ones, that wander off into her farm. A long time ago, she brought home and took care of a tiny sickly fox who got lost in the forest!

"A fox!" All the farm chickens exclaimed in fear. They couldn't help but think that the fox will eat them all, one day! But he never did. Who knew he would grow up to be really big and strong! He has been very good to them and is now happily living in the forest with his own family. He now voluntarily guards the coup and farm from the other foxes and forest beasts.

Because of this, all the other animals in the farm think that she is a peculiar hen! Some despise her unique way of thinking and too much kindness but most of them love her anyway! She doesn't dwell on the negativity around her. Instead, she focuses on what is good. She values honesty, hard work, education, kindness and courage.

When Mother Hen is not busy, she spends her time in the garden where she plants her flowers and vegetables. Mother Hen made Odette work and go to school everyday. She said, "You have to earn your keep, work hard and study, So that when you are old enough, you will be able to fend for yourself."

While the other chicks are playing, Odette studied hard at school and helped out at the coup and the field. When she wakes up in the morning, she helps make breakfast, cleans her bedroom and prepares for school. After her school work, she goes to the field and garden to help out in planting vegetables. And before the day ends, she helps prepare dinner for her and Mother Hen. The next day, she does it all over again.

She doesn't complain, but instead she is thankful. She thanks Mother Hen for the roof above her head, the food in her belly and her education.

But Odette misses her family everyday and cries every night. She couldn't understand why she was given away and made to live far away. Odette cries every night, heartbroken and betrayed.

One day, Mother Hen came home with a sick Baby Bird. Baby Bird was born so tiny and weak that his family abandoned him.

Papa Bird said that he needs strong birds and whoever can't keep up with the flock, will be left behind. Baby bird tried so hard but still couldn't keep up with their flying and passed out mid air and fell right in front of where Mother Hen was working in the garden.

Mother Hen and Odette tended to Baby Bird's needs and helped him become strong. They named him Little Sky. Soon Sky and Odette did the same thing everyday.

Odette said she didn't want to be given away again, so she worked very hard to please Mother Hen. She didn't want to be a burden and be left alone again. And Little Sky said that he doesn't want to be given away too! So he followed Odette's example. He follows her around and helps in the garden and at night he always prays with Odette before going to bed.

One night, Odette cried herself to sleep again. In her dream, appeared a bright light that spoke to her, "My child, what is the matter, why are you always crying yourself to sleep?"

Odette replied, "I miss my mother terribly, and my whole family. I don't understand why they left me. I feel angry! And guilty that I wasn't good enough for them. Why am I born this way?"

The bright light spoke again, "Dear Odette, have faith and do not be sad anymore. I am with you every minute and every second of your life. I am your mother, your father, your brother, your sister, your friend. I will never abandon you. I am always inside your heart." Odette woke up and wondered about her dream. "Who was that bright light that spoke to me? Hmm." She stretched her wings and went on with her usual daily activities.

The next night she dreamed again. She was happy to meet the light in her dream again. But this time the light revealed himself to Odette in a form of what seemed to be a round silver platter. He said, "Look in the mirror Odette and you shall see me." Odette looked in the mirror and saw her own image. She still couldn't understand what he meant.

Then, the light spoke to Odette once more. "Remember, Odette, you are brave and kind. I am always in your heart and in the hearts of those who love me and believe in me. I will never abandon you. Always believe in yourself and be of courage. I am God and I am always with you and I will protect you and bless you all the days of your life."

When Odette woke up the next day, she felt refreshed and happy. She pondered about her dream and realized that she is not alone after all! She has herself and God to rely on! So from now on, she will have faith in herself and believe that God is with her, living in her heart, as with all the other hearts in the world.

Therefore, she has to be mindful of the hearts around her and be careful not to hurt them because she doesn't want to hurt God who is living inside each heart. She decided to let go of her anger and self pity.

She got out of bed and looked at the mirror and saw that her feathers are sparkling! She looked so elegant! Little Sky saw her and he gasped! "You look like you have diamonds stuck in your feathers! You are so beautiful!", he said. She smiled and told them about her dreams. Mother Hen couldn't be more happy looking at Odette! Little Sky admired her even more and was inspired by her.

Mother Hen said, "Dear Odette and Little Sky, always remember that our outer self is a reflection of our hearts. So always keep God in your hearts and guard it from all evil and negativity! We shine brightly when our hearts are pure and true! Our appearances may be different but what is most important are the ones that we keep in our hearts."

"Odette, I have loved you ever since I met you because although you had sadness in your eyes I saw goodness in your heart. Little Sky, I love you too when you were tiny and weak because I saw courage in you! And to me, you are a gift that fell from the heavens! I don't want you two to be sad anymore, we have each other!" And she embraced her precious children whom she bore from her heart.

'After hearing this, Odette became even more grateful. Yes, it is true! She has Mother Hen and Little Sky too!'

Odette and Little Sky smiled and promised to always keep goodness in their hearts and protect it from all evil! And they all lived happily ever after with God firmly in their hearts.

CPSIA information can be obtained
at www.ICGtesting.com
Printed in the USA
BVHW021725030222
627988BV00015B/774